Bulletproof Blended Learning Design

Process, Principles and Tips

By

Frank Troha

Instructional Design Consultant

ISBN: 1-4107-8541-6 (e-book)
ISBN: 1-4107-8540-8 (Paperback)

This book is printed on acid free paper.

1stBooks - rev. 09/25/03

"I can't think of any publication that treats these two subjects - classroom and online instruction - in coordinated fashion as you do. Also, your concise treatment gets right to the important matters. For instructional designers in need of an effective, efficient approach to blended learning design, **Bulletproof Blended Learning Design** *is a must read."*

Jerrold E. Kemp, Ed.D.
Professor Emeritus of Instructional Technology, San Jose State University; Former President of the Association for Educational Communications and Technology (AECT); author/co-author of five education textbooks including *Designing Effective Instruction* (4th edition 2004, John Wiley & Sons); Learning Consultant to Silicon Valley companies (and others) for 30 years

"Anyone involved in developing blended learning materials - from instructional designers to project managers - should find Frank Troha's book of great value in providing an easy-to-follow formula for success."

Bob Little
Editor and Publisher of the Journal of the British Association for Open Learning (BAOL)

Disclaimer

This book's contents are based on the presumption that its readers are experienced designers of adult learning who have (at a minimum) designed successful classroom instruction, prepared instructional design documents (i.e., detailed course blueprints) and acquired a basic understanding of standard learning technologies, including instructional design models and their common components (e.g., audience analysis, learning objectives, content outline, evaluation methodology, etc.). Application of the information presented in this book is at the reader's risk.

Table of Contents

Why This Book

Anyone who has designed excellent instruction for the corporate classroom can easily learn how to design blended learning (typically a combination of traditional classroom instruction and e-learning). All that is needed is a *practical, proven* design model and some practice applying it.

This book offers such a model to corporate professionals who:

1. Oversee course design (or directly perform it) *and*

2. Have access to outside e-learning providers, typically hired to program and deploy online-course components.

The design model described in the following pages works remarkably well, however there is one caveat: **When designing a blended learning course, it is vitally important that you complete due diligence <u>before</u> consulting with outside providers.** Only by deliberately determining and confirming (with all internal colleagues involved) target audience characteristics, course learning objectives, subject matter to be addressed, likely constraints, etc. can you consistently:

1. Earn the trust and prerequisite support of your firm's decision makers, influencers and stakeholders.

2. Efficiently and accurately communicate project scope and requirements to prospective outside providers (and accurately and informatively answer their questions).

3. *Select the best outside provider for the job.*

4. Greatly minimize, if not avoid entirely, the consequences of inadequate project planning (e.g., substantial rework, delays and cost overruns).

5. Confidently lead and manage the project team (which includes the selected outside provider).

6. End up with a blended learning course that meets or exceeds all requirements.

1. Overview of the Recommended Model

The recommended model for blended learning design consists of three major, interrelated components:

1. Course Design Process
2. Guiding Principles
3. Success Tips

The **course design process** provides a step-by-step roadmap, starting with the gathering of basic information about the training need (i.e., standard training needs analysis and data collection) and <u>ending with an approved course design document (i.e., blueprint), which is later used to guide course development, delivery and evaluation</u>. (See Figure 1: Components of an Instructional Design Document, page 5.)

Guiding principles help shape fundamental course design decisions made throughout the course design process. The principles (derived from recent research) help answer questions, such as: "What's the optimal mix of self-study and live, instructor-led study?" "Should the instructor's role be primarily directive or facilitative?" "How important is it for learners to be able to interact with one another?" "If we integrate mentoring, can it be accomplished effectively by e-mail?" In total, the application of guiding principles should help ensure that your blended learning course is:

- Learner-centered
- Instructor-guided (as opposed to instructor-directed)

3

- Interactive
- Peer-collaborative
- Cost-effective

Success tips help ensure effective project management, particularly the optimization of all available resources, from project end to end. Examples:

- Establish and maintain ongoing communication with all decision makers, influencers and stakeholders associated with your project.
- Develop, confirm and apply precise, comprehensive provider-selection criteria.
- Communicate with the selected provider no less than once a week to ensure that milestones and quality standards (for both deliverables and client service) are being met.

When properly applied, the three major components of the blended learning design model (process, principles and tips) combine to provide a virtually no-fail, bulletproof approach. The following chapters address each component in detail.

Figure 1

Components of an Instructional Design Document

I. Course Title

II. Purpose Statement (the overall intent of the course succinctly stated)

III. Audience Description

IV. Duration

V. Prerequisites (if any)

VI. Learning Objectives

VII. Constraints

VIII. Content / Learning Activities Outline (For <u>each item of content</u> to be addressed, indicate how it would be conveyed to audience members and the estimated time required. *This is, by far, the longest section of the document.*)

IX.   Transfer of Learning Strategy

X.   Evaluation Strategy

Add any other sections that are needed to clearly and comprehensively communicate your design.

2. Course Design Process

Application of the following blended learning design process presumes a performance analysis has indicated the need for training, as opposed to another type of performance improvement intervention (e.g., process reengineering, job redesign, incentive program redesign, etc.).

BLENDED LEARNING DESIGN PROCESS

1. **Gather standard background information on the training need, just as you and your design team would if designing a course for classroom delivery.**

   Consider the job titles and functions of audience members, their geographic locations, total number to be trained within a given time frame, their level of interest in the subject matter, their likes/dislikes concerning learning activities experienced in the past, the gap between their level of current performance and the level of desired performance, what they need to come away with as a result of the training (i.e., knowledge, skills and attitude), *known and potential constraints* affecting any aspect of the <u>classroom</u> training from design to development to delivery, existing course-related documentation/content (if any), etc. In sum, perform the usual needs analysis and data collection with all internal parties involved, including subject matter experts.

2. **Precisely and accurately answer in writing: "What exactly do we want our audience to *know*, *do* and *feel* as a result of the training?"**

The list of specific, carefully worded outcomes or learning objectives should be prefaced by: "As a result of completing the training, participants should…"

Before proceeding to the next step in the process, *be sure to confirm the list of learning objectives with project decision makers, influencers, subject matter experts and any other appropriate parties.* (Because the objectives provide the basis for subsequent design activities, the need to verify their accuracy cannot be overstated.)

3. **Based on the confirmed learning objectives, outline the topics and subtopics that must be addressed by the training.**

Essentially, you and your design team (including any subject matter experts) should answer this question for each learning objective: *"If audience members are to accomplish this particular objective, what elements of content must they receive?"* The eventual output of this step should look like the table of contents in a thick textbook, i.e., highly detailed, comprehensive and logically organized.   Additionally, it should include an

"Introduction" unit (listing, e.g., attention-grabbing opener, audience expectations, learning objectives, agenda, housekeeping, etc.) and a "Conclusion" unit (listing, e.g., review of key points, action planning, course and instructor evaluation, etc.).

4. **Next to <u>each</u> item listed in the content outline, note the type of learning activity (e.g., brief lecture, case study, role play, simulation, game, etc.) that is best able to convey the item of content to your audience *in a traditional classroom setting*.**

The premise for noting classroom activities only at this point in the design process - instead of both classroom and online activities - is two-fold: 1) By working within the context of traditional classroom instruction - a venue with which you are familiar - you are establishing on paper the "ideal" learning experience: *live, face-to-face, instructor-facilitated and peer-collaborative.* <u>2) By virtue of having designed the "ideal" learning experience, you have a tangible blueprint ("Content / Learning Activities Outline") that you can - later in the process - systematically analyze from the standpoint of elements that could be delivered online (without compromising learning effectiveness) versus elements best left in a classroom setting.</u>

5. **Prepare a transfer of learning strategy that specifies what can be done *before*, *during* and *after* training to make it stick.**

This step is crucial. *If learning is not transferred from the place of learning to the place of work, there can be no positive return on investment.*

At this point, having produced a "Content / Learning Activities Outline", you and your design team would have a sense as to how the manager of a learner might encourage his/her on-the-job application of the content specified. For example, before training, the manager could review the course's learning objectives with the learner and discuss their relevance to his/her particular developmental needs. After training, the manager and learner might discuss, fine tune and commit to implementing an action plan drafted by the learner during training.

Additionally, a second look at the "Content / Learning Activities Outline" - from the standpoint of ensuring learning transfer - might trigger revisions, allowing for more (or better) in-class skill-building activities, instructor feedback and introduction of job aids (e.g., checklists, templates and memory joggers) for later use on-the-job.

Before proceeding, the overall transfer of learning strategy, which can include methods well beyond those noted above (e.g., linkage to annual performance review criteria), is bulleted out in three categories: *before*, *during* and *after* training.

6. **Prepare an evaluation strategy, outlining how the effectiveness of the training can be determined.**

A look back at the learning objectives and the "Content / Learning Activities Outline" can help answer these types of evaluation questions: "After confirming the accuracy of course materials with subject matter experts and other reviewers, will you test the relevance, value and appeal of course materials (in the final draft stage) by conducting 'walk-throughs' with a sampling of your target audience?" "Will you conduct a dry run so decision makers, influencers, training personnel and other appropriate parties can assess the course prior to rollout?" "After rollout, how will you measure the target audience's degree of satisfaction, actual learning and behavioral change?" "Given the nature of the training, can its impact on the organization be determined?" "If so, which metrics will you use?" "To get a true indication of the training's impact on the organization, how long after its delivery should measurement be made?"

An outline of the evaluation strategy is noted before proceeding.

7. **Organize all outputs of the preceding steps into an instructional design document (outlined in Figure 1, page 5).**

8. **Referring to the instructional design document's "Content / Learning Activities Outline", highlight items for potential online delivery.**

Since the intent of blended learning is to enhance learning by combining the best of both worlds - typically the 24/7 accessibility and global reach of online instruction with the live, face-to-face, human interaction of the traditional classroom - elements of the outline that appear to lend themselves to *self-study* online should be highlighted. *Such elements tend to include easy-to-interpret, straightforward information that is relatively easy for the learner to* *accurately* grasp on his/her own, e.g., key terms, process overviews, guiding principles, testimonials, self-assessment criteria, etc.*

9. **Brief all internal people involved with your project on the <u>preliminary</u> course design, elicit their feedback and gain approval to proceed.**

Getting buy-in from project decision makers, content experts and other key parties at this point in the design process is crucial.

First, this meeting should confirm whether you are on track in terms of what the target audience needs and what management wants. Second, by virtue of providing the opportunity for all involved to weigh in on the design (presented via the preliminary instructional design document), their cooperation and support are better ensured. And, third, <u>you (and they) can feel confident that the time has come to talk with outside providers who - after receiving a similar briefing - can indicate precisely *where*, *how* and *why* they would apply the most appropriate e-learning technologies (e.g., virtual-classroom instruction; simulations; collaboration venues, such as threaded discussions or online chat; online testing; online job aids; online coaching and mentoring; automated course administration and more)</u>.

10. **Meet with prospective outside providers to: a) learn precisely *where*, *how* and *why* they would apply e-learning technologies, and b) select the best provider for the job.**

Note: Prospective outside providers can be best identified by speaking with your counterparts in several or more organizations known to have successfully implemented e-learning and/or blended learning initiatives. To identify your counterparts, consult relevant professional associations, trade journal articles, websites devoted to e-learning and blended learning, etc.

By using the approved preliminary design document as a roadmap for your interviews with providers, your intentions and their ideas can be explored efficiently, accurately and thoroughly. Additionally, your use of a simple set of interview questions (prepared in advance) can help you further determine the best provider for the job. Issues such as past experience with similar courses and clients, quality standards, references, etc. need to be addressed in each of your meetings with prospective outside providers.

Key outputs of your meetings should include: 1) a clearer understanding as to which course elements should be delivered online versus offline, including rationale 2) a decision as to which provider seems most appropriate for the job and 3) which aspects of course development (i.e., the writing of course materials, such as case studies, simulations and assessments) can be accomplished using internal resources.

Note: Many of the outside experts' recommendations will require a clear understanding of your organization's current technological capabilities and limitations. Consequently, your organization's IT function should be represented at all such interviews.

11. <u>**With input from the outside provider of your choice**</u>, **prepare a revised instructional design document (i.e., the "Blended Learning Design Document"), detailing the most appropriate mix of online and offline learning activities.**

In the "Content / Learning Activities" section of your preliminary design document, make whatever edits and revisions you and the provider believe are needed to clearly and accurately indicate how <u>each</u> element of content *should* be delivered (whether online or offline) and the estimated time required to do so. Other sections of the design document (e.g., Duration [total online time vs. total classroom time], Constraints, Transfer of Learning Strategy, Evaluation Strategy, etc.) should also be adjusted, depending on decisions reached.

12. **Jointly present the blended learning design to all internal people involved with your project, elicit their feedback and ultimately gain approvals needed to proceed with course materials development.**

A key part of this briefing is comparing and contrasting the first approved design document (based on the "ideal" traditional classroom venue, but including the highlighting of certain elements for *possible* online delivery) with the second design document (based on the *optimal* blending of online and traditional classroom venues within the context of your organization's constraints and requirements). *As a result, the potential benefits to be gained from a blended approach should become apparent to all.*

Typical benefits include: reaching large numbers of learners "anywhere, anytime" and usually much faster (and cost-effectively) than multiple classroom deliveries alone could; optimizing expensive in-classroom time by limiting its use to course content requiring live, face-to-face interaction among participants and instructor; automating course administration, such as learner registration, testing and record keeping; and reducing overall training expenditures.

Once the blended learning design is approved, next steps (relating to logistical issues) are discussed in terms of roles, responsibilities and timing. Issues include negotiating and contracting with the outside provider you selected and recommend, project scheduling, the internal process to be followed when reviewing drafts of course materials, etc.

As indicated in the preceding chapter, the blended learning design process described above does not exist in a vacuum. **Guiding principles, which follow, need to be applied <u>during</u> the design** process, if the resultant course is to be effective from an instructional standpoint.

3. Guiding Principles

Too often questions raised during blended learning design are answered on the basis of intuition instead of fact. The following findings - culled from numerous recent studies conducted by U.S. universities, professional associations and government agencies - can help ensure the integrity of your design and, ultimately, the effectiveness of your course.

As you review the following list, *four overarching principles for the design of blended learning should become apparent: learner-centered, instructor-guided (as opposed to instructor-directed), interactive and peer-collaborative.* A fifth imperative, cost-effective, is a given.

SUMMARY OF RESEARCH FINDINGS

1. Learning is enhanced when instructors see themselves as active guides to learning and learners perceive themselves as owners of their learning, actively analyzing, questioning, discussing and developing knowledge and skill.

2. Giving learners control over when and how they develop knowledge and skill tends to increase the individualization of instruction, a sense of personal responsibility for learning and learning efficiency. (However, until learners are able and willing

to take control, expecting them to be self-directed is likely to hinder rather than enhance learning.)

3. Web-based instruction can and should enable the delivery of course content tailored to each learner's particular learning style and preferences.

4. Learner-centered approaches should be extended to team-centered activities whenever a learning activity lends itself to a group effort (e.g., learning cannot or should not be accomplished by individual effort, or the learning objectives pertain to communication, teamwork or some other group-functioning skill).

5. An effective orientation to blended learning enhances three types of interactivity required for optimal learning: learner-to-instructor, learner-to-learner and learner-to-instructional materials. The orientation should consist of instructor's welcome, learning objectives, course outline, types of learning activities to expect, how learning will be evaluated, course schedule, instructor's expectations, contact information and next steps (e.g., learners are to communicate their own expectations and complete an ice-breaker assignment).

6. Explaining to learners the importance, means and desired frequency of interaction at the outset of a course increases the amount of interaction.

7. Completion rates of online courses are substantially improved when participants are provided with a comprehensive orientation to online learning, timely and personalized feedback from the instructor, high-level technical support and well-designed, instructor-mediated learning activities.

8. Online collaboration improves learning effectiveness by allowing learners to reflect, present individual positions, debate, construct new paradigms and otherwise interact with each other. Additionally, anxiety levels tend to be reduced as a sense of community is developed.

9. Mentoring of participants by the instructor, course graduates or other qualified individuals enhances learning and can be accomplished successfully via e-mail.

10. Learners tend to be highly sensitive to system response time. If perceived as slow, it can seriously impair the effectiveness of instruction. Findings include:

- To maintain participants' attention, they should be informed when any download requires more than a 10-second wait.

- When directly manipulating objects on the screen (e.g., disassembling a piece of equipment represented in 3D), the time between moving the cursor and seeing the result on the screen should be under 0.1 seconds. (If slower, the lag time becomes a source of frustration.)

- When clearing a spreadsheet or turning a page, for example, a lag time of up to one second is acceptable. However, waiting more than one second tends to discourage learners from exploring options they otherwise would (e.g., supplemental materials).

11. The most effective blending of live instruction (synchronous) with self-paced learning (asynchronous) appears to be one hour of live instruction for every four hours of self-paced learning.

12. Though often underestimated, asynchronous learning strongly supports a collaborative learning environment by enabling every learner to contribute when, where and at a pace that is personally preferable. Additionally, the quality of learner contributions made asynchronously (and expressed in writing) tends to be higher than those made during live sessions.

13. Real time chats on a topic generate more responses per learner than asynchronous discussions. However, asynchronous discussions foster deeper analysis and evaluation of ideas.

14. For online instructors to be effective, they need to have input into anticipating and addressing likely learner questions and issues during course design, be responsive (e.g., provide learners with timely feedback on coursework), create a psychologically safe learning environment, be conversational in tone, confirm that all online and off-line activities are clearly explained and understood, actively guide learning (e.g., pose timely questions, correct misconceptions, focus/refocus discussions), encourage learners to go beyond assimilating existing knowledge to creating their own personal and group knowledge, and foster a sense of community with and among learners.

15. Learners should be encouraged and given every opportunity to interact with peers, instructor(s), guest experts and the instructional material itself. However, it is vitally important to provide clear instruction and guidance on how to do so within the context of available online learning tools and techniques.

16. Determining whether a sense of community truly exists among learners requires evidence of learners knowing one another,

discussing common interests, disclosing personal information, sharing tasks, helping one another, contributing towards the accomplishment of common goals, respecting each other and taking risks.

17. To help ensure the participation of all learners, learning activities need to include verifiable interactions with course materials, other learners and the instructor (e.g., reporting results upon completing independent and team-based activities).

18. Integrating teamwork on actual projects with online learning activities further engages participants and thereby enhances learning. Such collaboration can be accomplished through video and computer conferencing, e-mail, sharing of documents, etc.

Taken collectively, the above findings indicate blended learning needs to be learner-centered, instructor-guided, interactive and collaborative, if it is to be truly effective. Taken individually, the findings comprise a quick-reference tool - a sounding board of sorts - particularly helpful when making challenging design decisions.

4. Success Tips

Leading a blended learning initiative (that includes online learning) is a relatively new, complex and high-stakes challenge. Whether you are heading up a project or serving as a key contributor, the following project management tips apply.

1. **Identify all decision makers, influencers and stakeholders, and involve them from the very start.**

   The success of your course will depend just as much on the input, cooperation and support of various key individuals at various levels in your organization as it will on the work you and your design team perform.

   Before you begin the design process, take the time to identify all internal parties either directly or indirectly connected with the course to be designed. Top management, IT, Human Resources, the managers to whom target audience members report and your organization's legal department represent some typical constituents. Once all parties have been identified, personally meet with them to discuss the nature of your project, its importance to the organization and ways in which they can help contribute to its success.

By involving all parties concerned sooner rather than later, you are likely to gain and keep their support throughout the life cycle of the project.

2. **Precisely define - and get agreement on - roles and responsibilities from the get-go.**

Too often it is erroneously assumed all internal parties involved in a project understand what is expected of them. This recent statement by a senior instructional designer illustrates the point: "When we asked our internal subject matter experts to review our work for accuracy, they instead ripped it apart from a design standpoint and said we'd need to redo everything." He went on to say bruised egos, lengthy delays and other kinds of negative fallout ensued.

To help prevent such situations, be sure roles and responsibilities are specified, understood and accepted before design-related work begins.

3. **Carefully select the right provider for the job.**

Procuring the technical services needed to prepare and deliver online-learning components is fraught with challenges. To greatly improve the odds of selecting the most appropriate provider:

- Develop a precise, comprehensive set of selection criteria (e.g., past experience addressing similar subject matter for similar organizations, fee structure, quality standards, references, etc.) before meeting with any prospective providers. And be sure to apply the same set of well thought out selection criteria to each prospective provider (to prevent having to compare apples with oranges later on).

- Prepare a list of prospective outside providers. As previously mentioned, you can identify them by speaking with your counterparts in several or more organizations known to have successfully implemented e-learning and/or blended learning initiatives. (To identify your counterparts, consult relevant professional associations, trade journal articles, websites devoted to e-learning and blended learning, etc.)

- When interviewing prospective providers, use the preliminary instructional design document first, followed by your selection criteria. As explained in Chapter 2: Course Design Process, the preliminary instructional design document should enable you to clearly and efficiently communicate what you have in mind to prospective providers, as well as respond informatively to any questions they ask you. Further, the document should position you to pose this crucial question:

"To take our design to the next level, what exactly would you recommend and why?" Only if the response to that question were satisfactory, would you apply your set of selection criteria by asking, for example: "How long would it take your organization to deliver what we discussed?" "How much would it cost roughly?" "Has your firm served companies in our industry?" "Have you developed courses on the same subject matter as ours?" "May we speak with some of the clients you're currently working with?"

By virtue of properly using your preliminary design document and set of selection criteria in your meetings with prospective providers, you are very likely to identify the provider best suited for the job.

4. **Strive for continuous communication with all parties associated with your project, <u>especially the selected outside provider</u>.**

A successful blended learning initiative requires careful project planning, solid instructional design, the development of all instructional components based on an approved design document, ongoing attention to project management issues (e.g., budget, scheduling and communications), various course reviews and evaluations prior to launch, deployment of the learning, and ongoing evaluation and maintenance of the entire learning system. *With so many opportunities for misunderstanding, the importance of continuous communication with everyone concerned with your project cannot be overstated.*

Particularly crucial is establishing and maintaining a wide-open channel of communication between you and the outside provider. As soon as practicable, meet everyone assigned to your project at the provider firm, and make a special effort to get to know your primary contact there. Before work begins in earnest, be sure to determine service standards relating to communications, e.g., *meet at least once a week*, maintain a project management website to be updated daily, return all phone calls within 24 hours, etc.

5. **Avoid mistakes by learning from the experiences of others.**

Your counterparts in other organizations who have "been there and done that" can be an invaluable source of practical information. They can help you identify reliable providers, fine tune your provider-selection criteria and share critical lessons learned, ranging from negotiating contracts to overseeing the work of providers. Be sure to establish, cultivate *and benefit from* such relationships by asking for assistance as needed and, of course, reciprocating as best you can.

Frank Troha

The above success tips - combined with the other two components of the recommended model (process and principles) - offer you a virtually no-fail, bulletproof approach to the design of blended learning.

5. Why This Model Works

The recommended model for the design of blended learning is effective because it:

- Conveniently builds on what most *experienced* instructional designers tend to do very well, i.e., design classroom instruction.

- Requires the design team to thoroughly grasp their project's likely scope and basic requirements as a prerequisite to preparing and presenting a *preliminary* design for internal feedback and approval.

- Employs checks and balances including confirmation of learning objectives, preparation and approval of a preliminary design document, consistent application of prepared provider-selection criteria, etc.

- Taps the expertise of several (or more) outside providers who are asked to explain how the approved preliminary design can be taken to the "next level", i.e., the optimal blended learning solution.

- Helps ensure the hiring of the best provider for the job through the consistent application of prepared selection criteria coupled with the quality of each provider's design recommendations.

- Results in a Blended Learning Design Document that *details* the most optimal blending of online and classroom instruction.

- By virtue of comparing the preliminary design document with the Blended Learning Design Document, clearly reveals - to all internal parties concerned - the potential benefits to be gained by implementing a blended solution.

- Facilitates clear communication, cooperation and support among all key parties involved from project start to finish.

- Encourages benefiting from lessons learned by counterparts who have "been there and done that".

Perhaps you have experienced the following situation firsthand. An organization requests proposals from outside providers before fundamental course design and project management issues have been adequately defined. As a result, the organization's decision makers receive vague proposals, offering few details about what they can expect to receive for their money. Anxious to get started, they contract with one of the outside providers and begin work. Within a week or two, various parties involved with the project find themselves at odds over a host of crucial course design and project management issues, ranging from learning objectives to IT requirements to course maintenance. Inevitably it is realized: *There has to be a better way.* (And, of course, there is.)

An Invitation

Because instructional designers vary in their work requirements and personal preferences, there are no universally accepted models for the design of classroom instruction, e-learning or blended learning. Consequently, the author has no illusions about the applicability of his blended learning design model *precisely as presented in this book*. Odds are some steps, principles and tips recommended simply do not apply to your particular situation or require your adaptation.

Certainly you are encouraged to make whatever adjustments you must to make the recommended model work for you. And you are invited to share your comments and questions concerning any aspect of its structure or application. Please write to: frank@franktroha.com.

Appendix

Snapshot of the Course Design Process

1. Gather standard background information on the training need, just as you and your design team would if designing a course for the traditional classroom.

2. Precisely and accurately answer in writing: "What exactly do we want our audience to know, do and feel as a result of the training?"

3. For each objective, answer in writing: "In order for our audience to attain this objective, what content needs to be addressed?"

4. Next to each item listed in the content outline, note the type of learning activity that is best able to convey the item of content in a traditional classroom setting.

5. Develop a transfer of learning strategy that specifies what can be done before, during and after training to make it stick.

6. Prepare an evaluation strategy, outlining how the effectiveness of the training can be determined.

7. Organize all outputs of the preceding steps into an instructional design document (outlined in Figure 1, page 5).

8. Referring to the instructional design document's "Content / Learning Activities Outline", highlight items that appear well suited for online delivery.

9. Using the instructional design document as a discussion document, brief all internal people involved with your project on the preliminary course design, elicit their feedback and gain approval to proceed.

10. Meet with prospective outside providers to: a) learn precisely *where*, *how* and *why* they would apply e-learning technologies to optimize the instructional efficiency and effectiveness of your design, and b) select the best provider for the job.

11. With input from the outside provider of your choice, prepare a revised instructional design document (i.e., the "Blended Learning Document"), detailing the most appropriate mix of online and offline learning activities.

12. Jointly present the blended learning design to all internal people involved with your project, elicit their feedback and ultimately gain approvals needed to begin course materials development.

About the Author

For the past 20-plus years, Frank Troha has served the instructional design needs of leading U.S.-based corporations. His proven methods and techniques have been cited in the *United States Distance Learning Association Journal, Journal of the British Association for Open Learning, Learning & Training Innovations, Workforce Management, Business & Legal Reports, Expresso-emprego, Training* and Tom Peters' website *(www.tompeters!)*.

Frank began his corporate career as Senior Instructional Designer with Control Data Professional Services, a pioneer in computer-based learning technologies. He later managed instructional design services at Philip Morris USA and Juran Institute. In 1983, he established his consultancy, specializing in the design of customized management, sales and technical training programs.

Frank is also Adjunct Associate Professor of Instructional Design at Fordham University Graduate School of Education where, for the past nine years, he has taught his specialty to corporate human resource development professionals.

Frank lives and works near New York City. His office is located in The Landmark (former Lifesavers Candy factory), Port Chester, New York.

Printed in the United States
22618LVS00001B/1441-1443